The Meditation of Little Richard

Pasanno Burch

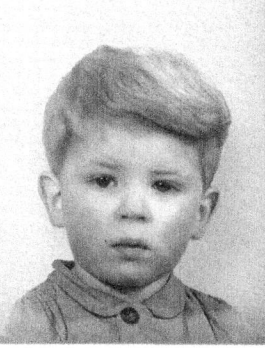

PREFACE

Welcome to this humble collection of reflections and teachings, born of a journey intertwined with threads of life and meditation. Within these pages, you will find the thoughts and guiding light of Pasanno, a name bestowed upon Richard by one of his teachers to enhance his meditation practice.

Little Richard was born in Rochford Hospital on May 25th 1949. His mother left him shortly after his birth as she was unable to care for him. He imagined her leaving the room, pausing for a final glance before departing,* leaving him feeling very unhappy. After two weeks, he was adopted, and it would be another fifty years before he reunite with his birth mother, but that is a story for another time.

As you leaf through these pages, you are invited to traverse a landscape of meditation, mindfulness, and the gentle art of living with purpose.

* This memory did not originate from early childhood; rather, it surfaced during a meditation retreat. When Richard later reunited with his birth mother, she confirmed the validity of the experience.

From the early yearnings of Little Richard to the seasoned wisdom of Pasanno, the essence of this book resonates with a profound desire to help others in their quest for inner peace and clarity.

Embraced by the warmth of shared practice and the spirit of community, these words were crafted not as lofty doctrines but as practical companions for the meditator's path.

With each passage shared with the Sangha, a beacon of guidance illuminated the way for those seeking solace and understanding amidst the complexities of life.

This book stands as a testament to the power of compassion and the unyielding light that shines within each of us. May it serve as a gentle companion on your own journey toward self-discovery and inner harmony.

LITTLE RICHARD'S FIRST MEMORIES

When Little Richard was about two years old, he stood in the garden at his parents' flat in Southend-on-Sea, Essex. His parents and baby brother were sitting at a table, drinking and eating, while Little Richard wandered off down the path towards the flat. As he gazed up at the beautiful blue sky adorned with fluffy white clouds, a sense of serenity washed over him. It was a moment unlike any other he had experienced before.

In that instance, a profound realization struck him – the beauty of the sky had never captured his thoughts in such a way. His childlike sense of freedom seemed to slip away, leaving him feeling a loss he couldn't quite comprehend. Despite his desperate attempts to reclaim that feeling, it remained elusive, a fleeting moment of pure innocence now out of reach. As he began to develop his sense of self, he noticed two distinct paths before him.

To his left, a misty tunnel beckoned, a reminder of where he had come from in a realm before this life. To his right, a clearer path emerged, signalling the journey he must embark upon to rediscover that selfless place he had inadvertently left behind. Little did he know that this quest for innocence and happiness would span a lifetime of self-discovery, leading him back to that state of selflessness and joy.

This transformative experience ignited a passion within Little Richard to not only heal himself but also to guide others on their own paths to freedom. It laid the foundation for the profound insights and teachings that would later be shared in the pages of this book.

LITTLE RICHARD'S DREAM

When he was a young boy, Little Richard had a prophetic dream. In this dream, he found himself on a distant planet in another part of the universe, where the constellations differed from those on Earth.

The daytime sky was a breathtaking sight, painted in pastel pinks, lilacs, and vibrant blues, creating a mesmerizing tapestry that greeted the planet's inhabitants each morning. Tall buildings with heavenly arching spires adorned the towns, showcasing the architectural brilliance of the planet's residents.

Despite the beauty that surrounded them, the people on this planet seemed blind to it, consumed by their daily routines and responsibilities. Young Richard was in awe of the extraordinary buildings, but his attempts to point out their magnificence to passers-by were met with confusion and dismissal. He couldn't understand why others were indifferent to the beauty that unfolded before them each day.

Upon waking from his dream, Richard carried with him a sense of enlightenment, knowing that there was more to the world than meets the eye. Though initially too shy to share his experience with others, he eventually gained the confidence to speak about the profound truth he had discovered. The happiness and insight from his dream stayed with him for days, shaping his perspective on life.

As he grew older, Richard shared his dream with friends, emphasizing the importance of looking beyond the illusions of the world. While some were uninterested, he remained steadfast in his belief that he had valuable teachings to offer, particularly in the realm of meditation practices.

MEETING AJAHN CHAH

In my late teens, my mother borrowed some books from the library on yoga that I found very interesting. I was reading a lot of books such as *The Devil Rides Out* by Dennis Wheatley.

I was very keen on astronomy and even built an observatory at the bottom of my parent's garden to house my large telescope. I thought that the answer to all my suffering might be out there in the night sky. While gazing at the stars, I often felt that I was a part of them and at one of the universe.

When I was twenty, a work colleague mentioned that he was visiting The Hampstead Buddhist Vihara at Belsize Park in London, and was very excited about the place. Because I was shy, it took me a while to pluck up the courage to go. In those days, a person had to have an interview before they were accepted. It didn't take long for me to realized that this community and practice were what I had been looking for since I was two years old.

I loved the Vihara; it had a wonderful soothing spiritual atmosphere and, in the garden, there were meditation cells where one could undertake personal retreats.

After a few years, an American monk called Venerable Sumedho arrived from Thailand to help set up an English Sangha following instructions from his famous teacher Ajahn Chah.

Ajahn Chah had established several forest monasteries in Thailand and a few western monks who had followed his teachings had come to Hampstead. Ajahn Brahm* was one of those who visited, but at the time I was unaware of who he was.

After a while, it was rumoured that Ajahn Chah was coming to visit Hampstead. My heart skipped a beat, at the thought of meeting this wonderful teacher.

Some laypeople had offered their house for Ajahn Chah to give a talk. It had a magnificent view over Hampstead Heath through a large patio door. There was a commotion on the stairs outside, and Ajahn Chah entered. He was a small, stocky man with a physique that was perfect for meditation.

Ajahn Chah began to speak, and the monk who accompanied him translated for the audience.

* Ajahn Brahm, is a British Theravada Buddhist monk and meditation teacher. He is the abbot of Bodhinyana Monastery in Western Australia and the Spiritual Director of the Buddhist Society of Western Australia.

After about two hours, it was time for me to leave. Maybe it was because of the translation, but I can honestly say that the talk disappointed me.

As I boarded the train for the journey home, I felt rather let down, and as we pulled into my station, the sky darkened. It was nearly as black as night as the thunder and lightning rolled in. The rain was torrential and I opened my umbrella. I approached a man sheltering under a tree who was getting very wet and asked if he would like to share my umbrella, but he said he was nearly home, and we parted company.

My shyness had always prevented me from openly asking a question like that of a stranger. I reflected on what had happened, and it was clear that Ajahn Chah's presence had deeply effected me. I went into bliss and in the following days I remained very happy.

Ajahn Chah was a truly great teacher, and when he died in Thailand in 1992, over a million people visited his body.

I am *very* pleased that I went to his talk.

AT THE TIP OF YOUR NOSE

THE FOUR NOBLE TRUTHS

The potential for enlightenment is always in the present moment, right at the tip of your nose.

However, we often find it challenging to attain this freedom from suffering because we are attached to things in this realm. Unknowingly, we leave behind our freedom. As our mind moves away from its place of rest and peace, suffering arises. This movement of the mind with attachment is the root cause of suffering. When the mind reflects upon itself like a mirror, the path is revealed. By observing the mind with mindfulness, we can reach the end of all suffering, leading us to the Noble Eightfold Path.

NOBLE EIGHTFOLD PATH

1. Right View
2. Right Thought
3. Right Speech
4. Right Action
5. Right Livelihood
6. Right Effort
7. Right Mindfulness
8. Right Stillness of mind

So, what is happening is that birth and death are occurring every moment. If we have desires, and attachments (this is ego), we are born again. In fact, we are born and die every moment. For enlightenment to occur, we need to be selfless, we need to let go, and we must not attach.

One could say that we are already enlightened, but we have not yet realized it! It's like a beautiful clear pool in the forest; there is mud at the bottom, but we keep stirring the waters.

The path to enlightenment may take several lifetimes to achieve, but with dedicated practice, the veil of illusion is peeled back, revealing the clear pool.

I AM NOT WORTHY OF THIS HAPPINESS

PART 1

This was a real challenge for me when I first started meditating. Whenever my mind was calm and peaceful, a happy feeling would bubble up, but I would immediately think, "I don't deserve to feel this happy." My thoughts raced faster than lightning, pushing that happy feeling deep down inside me until it was destroyed. I'd feel frustrated, thinking, "This isn't fair! I want to feel happy." But I had no idea why this kept happening several times a month.

Then, during one meditation session, it finally clicked. The reason behind it all was my low self-esteem – or to put it bluntly, I didn't love myself. In fact, I think I might have even hated myself. As a father of two wonderful sons, I was scared of everything, including them.

Despite practicing *Vipassana* (Insight meditation) for a few years, I realized that the missing piece was showing kindness to myself and others. That's when I started practicing *metta*, or loving-kindness meditation. I would repeat the words, "May I be happy, may I be at peace, may I be free from all suffering," as my teacher once advised me during a retreat.

Placing my hands on my heart while saying those words made a huge difference. The feeling of unworthiness disappeared, replaced by a profound happiness and a sense of peace. Much of my fear melted away, and I experienced a level of happiness I had never known before. It felt like I had been searching for this happiness for ages, even though I had always known deep down that it was within me all along – just as it is within everyone.

One helpful practice that I recommend is this: when faced with difficult emotions like fear, regret, or shame, take a moment to slow down, place your hand on your heart, and say to yourself, "May I be kind to myself in this moment." This simple act can help us connect with the present moment and realize that it is not solely based on our sensory perceptions.

JUST ASK

We all face challenges, habits and conflicts that we wish to overcome and let go of. Allow me to share some strategies that have helped me navigate past difficulties.

These difficulties included moments like encountering children at a bus stop, seeing my reflection in a shop window and feeling unworthy of happiness when I was joyful. I used to prefer sitting at the back during talks and was hesitant to ask questions. I was afraid of just about everything, including my own young sons. This pattern didn't just need to change – it had to stop!

I was attached to all the negativity, but the most extraordinary thing was, I felt safe in the suffering. To develop a more selfless life frightened me somewhat, because what would happen to Richard if all this stuff disappeared?

The ego can fight back by sapping your energy and leaving you feeling fatigued. It can send you along an unskillful path and convince you intellectually that you have *the* answer.

This mind training can be quite a challenge. Once while on a retreat, the teacher led us through a loving-kindness meditation. We were asked to place our hands over our chest and get in touch, not with the physical heart, but the emotional human heart. This practice helped me see and release just a little bit of my true nature – just a bit – revealing an egoless place where I could heal Little Richard.

When the mind is quiet and the feeling of 'me' and 'mine' begins to fade, you can just ask the right question and the true answer can emerge through wisdom. The mind will then have the opportunity to reveal a beautiful vision and send you along a skilful path, without you even realizing that you have left your meditation.

I AM NOT WORTHY OF THIS HAPPINESS

PART 2

Why did I feel so happy all of a sudden? There must be a reason behind it. It all traces back to my school days many years ago.

When I was ten, I attended a boarding school as a day student. Unfortunately, I was bullied by several children. Every day, as I approached the school gates, they would be waiting for me, ready to kick, punch, and hurl insults. Their actions made me so miserable that I couldn't help but cry, which only seemed to encourage them further.

Reflecting on my recent meditation retreat, a moment stood out when my teacher instructed us to place our hands on our hearts and recite words of loving-kindness: "May I be happy, may I be at peace, may I be free from all suffering." It dawned on me that I had been carrying the pain inflicted by those bullies for many years. I had unknowingly projected that hurt onto my children and other men, viewing them as the bullies in my mind, even though logically they were not. My emotions were clouding my judgment, and I found myself fearful of them.

The meditation experience was truly transformative because it helped break that cycle of negativity. I realized that I would never have to endure that pain again. A sense of healing washed over that wounded part of my heart, and a new-found wisdom began to illuminate from within.

This is the profound impact of loving-kindness meditation, a practice taught by the Buddha over 2,500 years ago.

A CLOSER LOOK AT SUFFERING

WHAT IS THE CAUSE AND WHAT IS THE WAY OUT?

WE NEED TO DEFINE WHAT IS GOING ON.

A skilful way to begin is to change the way we say things in our mind. Take fear and worry as examples. These are caused by identifying with our ego and attaching to our ideas and desires.

Recognize that fear has arisen and avoid saying "I'm afraid," instead try "Fear has arisen."

Recognize that worry has arisen and avoid saying "I'm worried," instead try "Worry has arisen."

When we begin to change our words, fear and worry will subside and we will be left with a sense of spaciousness.

INTROSPECT: Take a few deep breaths and bring your attention inside.

EXAMINE: Look at your feelings deeply, their causes and their nature.

EFFECTS: First, whereabouts in the body does the feeling reside? Then, how does it feel inside the body? What is it's nature? It was not there a few minutes ago. Where did it come from and where did it go?

Intuitively every human being has the capacity to locate and examine their feelings and then ... let go.

VISUALISATION MEDITATION

Slowly and carefully close your eyes, you are about to travel back in time over 2,500 years ...

... You find yourself barefoot, walking slowly and mindfully in a lush, exotic forest. You are surrounded by tall trees and colourful flowers.

The air is filled with heady perfume and enchanting birdsong, and with each step the soft grass tickles your toes.

As you walk onwards, you realise that the birds have stopped singing, creating an oasis of calm beneath the canopy.

A little way off you see a clearing where a few monks have gathered in a semi-circle. They are waiting for the Buddha to give a talk. You sit quietly behind them and as a rainbow-coloured aura descends and envelopes the clearing, you sense that the Buddha is very close. The Buddha appears and settles in the lotus position. He begins to talk and as you listen, your heart is filled with joy.

When The Buddha has finished, He stands and beckons you to come forward. He embraces you and you are filled with a bliss and happiness that you have never experienced before. "If you keep practicing," He says, "one day you will come to understand the truth."

You wander back through the forest, thinking about the wonderful encounter. ...

... Slowly, you open your eyes and smile, still filled with a bliss and happiness that you have never experienced before.

TEN TIPS FOR BETTER MEDITATION PRACTICE
MEDITATION SHOULD BE FUN, NOT BORING

1. Our thoughts wander because minds always seem to want something interesting to happen. "Oh no, not another half an hour of watching the breath!" We then feel sleepy and the next thing we know we are throwing up the z's.

2. We usually begin mindful breathing with the in-breath, so try changing this by beginning with the out breath.

3. Hold your breath for a few seconds, the thoughts may stop.

4. Try sitting in a different location or position. Simply turning to face the other way can help.

5. Make sure your back is straight and your head is not drooping forward.

6 Keep your attention on the breath-body, following the breath from the tip of your nose through the body and back out again.

7 Using incense can help us to sense the breath more easily. My favourite is sandalwood.

8 Imagine that in the past, where you are sitting right now, someone came to enlightenment.

9 In your mind's eye, imagine that you are sitting with monks and nuns in the forest or with a famous teacher.

10 Let go and don't try too hard ... step back from the thoughts.

HOW TO MAINTAIN DAILY MEDITATION PRACTICE

To maintain a daily meditation practice, consistency is key. Set a specific time each day for meditation, start with a few minutes and gradually increase, create a dedicated space, use reminders or meditation apps, be patient with yourself, and stay committed even on busy days.

I always remind myself that one day there might be an illness that strikes me down which would mean that I couldn't do my meditation.

The world and all living beings are impermanent, my death can come without warning. This body will be a corpse. Thinking this, every day I will examine myself.

The laws of kamma and cause and effect cannot be escaped. I must try and cut desire and attachment and realize the Dhamma.

So strive forth with earnestness.

EXPERIMENT

While meditating one morning, I had a thought that could potentially help fellow practitioners. What if I tried holding onto thoughts instead of letting them go, just to see what happens?

I decided to experiment by holding onto whatever sensations came through my six senses. The first thing that arose was the feeling of my teeth touching each other in my mouth.

However, after a short while, this sensation slipped away and was replaced by another. For a brief moment, my entire existence was solely focused on the sense of touch. There was no sense of 'me' or 'mine', just the sensation itself. Breaking down existence in this way allowed me to see the impermanent nature of reality.

The illusion of permanence shattered, and concepts like self, soul or ego dissolved. It became clear that nothing truly belongs to us. If it did, we could hold onto happiness indefinitely, but reality doesn't work that way.

Understanding this impermanence, I returned to my meditation practice, continuing to let go of thoughts, knowing that everything is subject to change.

THE WARDROBE

I decided to move my bedroom to another room for a change. We have lived in our present house for fifty years, and a different view out of the window would be good.

This will be quite a project because the old wardrobe would have to be shifted before a new fitted one was assembled by the builders. My wife and I worked hard to get parts of the wardrobe down the stairs and into the garden.

Afterward, I sat down, and my heart rate was going quite fast. I thought that I must have overdone it because this never usually happens.

The next day my heart was still beating too quickly. I thought I must be run down. This feeling went on for quite a few days. One morning when my alarm clock went off, I was frightened by it. This was very odd because I don't usually suffer from fear.

I sat down in meditation to do some retrospective mindfulness of what had happened over the last few days. The wardrobe removal is where it all began. It was then that I remembered my thoughts. "It is hard work changing this home." Just after those thoughts came a very quick subtle thought about "homework" in my mind.

My mind sensed a similar situation about homework from my school days. My parents would always force me to finish my homework, which I hated. They were only trying to help me pass my exams, but I wanted to be an artist. So my fast heartbeat was because I was anxious about getting my homework wrong and being caned when I got to school by a teacher who was a sadist.

When I realized what was going on, the next stage was some loving-kindness toward my parents, who were only trying to help. The anxiousness disappeared, which was a great relief.

Next time something like this happens to you, don't forget the power of retrospective mindfulness and loving-kindness meditation.

GRATITUDE

Last night, just by chance, I watched a YouTube film about people who had received a cochlear implant, which is an electronic device that improves hearing. It can be an option for people with severe hearing loss from the inner ear.

The first film was about a lady of about twenty years old. It was wonderful to watch her burst into tears of joy as the doctor turn on the implant. Some tiny babies had such gorgeous smiles when they could hear for the first time.

The next film was about blind people having operations to restore their sight. One story which touched me was of a lady of about twenty-five years old, who only had an inch of viable focus. Because of this, the children of her school saw her as different and would regularly push her to the ground and kick her. It took about two years from the operation for her to be able to see clearly.

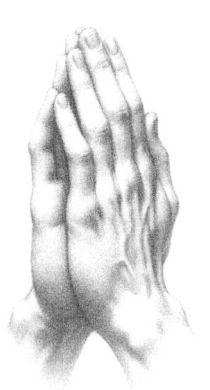

This morning, before meditation, two beautiful ducks flew through the garden. I stopped and looked. This inspired me to say "thank you," for my six senses, being healthy, having a roof over my head and for a warm bed to sleep in. I must say thank you for enough food and loving friends and family. I am truly grateful to be blessed with this. So every day, I try to practice gratitude.

BODY AND MIND

In the past, we viewed the body as something beautiful, with its attractive outer appearance. However, the human heart often harboured darkness, filled with anxiety, fear, anger, jealousy, desire and depression.

When we perceive the human body as something more than neutral, the human heart reveals its true beauty. It can experience genuine peace, remaining calm and tranquil.

The natural state of the human mind is one of stillness and peace. Yet, we tend to cling to things and agitate our thoughts. It is essential to simply let go and remind ourselves that none of this truly belongs to us.

SOME HISTORY

In my late teens, my mother borrowed some books from the library on yoga that I found very interesting. I was reading a lot of books such as *The Devil Rides Out* by Dennis Wheatley. I was very keen on astronomy; I even had a large telescope and had built an observatory at the bottom of my parent's garden. I thought that the answer to all my suffering might be out there in the stars. One night while looking through my telescope, I felt I had left this world behind and was right next to the stars.

When I was twenty, a work colleague mentioned that he was visiting a Buddhist Vihara in Hampstead, and was very excited about the place. Because I was so shy, it took me a while to pluck up the courage to go. In those days, a person had to have an interview before they were accepted. There were meditation cells in the back garden and I realized that this was what I had been looking for since I was two years old.

One evening, a monk announced that he was leaving, which left me very upset, feeling like I was on my own again. A few years later, the great teacher Ajahn Chah came to visit. He brought Ajahn Sumedho and some other monks as well. Chithurst Monastery was later established in Sussex.

HEALED BY A DREAM

The other day, I was fortunate to land a job creating several drawings for a children's poetry book. I had to illustrate a Diplodocus playing the guitar, a grandpa struggling with a tomato ketchup bottle, a hedgehog, and various other characters. Despite the heavy workload, I dedicated long hours over four days to this project and thoroughly enjoyed the opportunity to contribute to a children's book.

The following morning, upon waking, I found myself feeling anxious again, with my heart racing. I turned to meditation to explore the cause of my unease. Reflecting on the past few days, I recalled the children's poetry book. This triggered memories of my schooling, particularly my English class taught by a sadistic teacher who took pleasure in causing distress to students. He was a large, perspiring man who would punish us harshly for any mistakes.

One particular memory stood out – the time he had assigned us William Wordsworth's poem "She Dwelt Among the Untrodden Ways." to memorize.

I can still recall parts of it today. Those who didn't give a smooth recitation would face punishment with a ruler. I was so frightened by this that I couldn't recite the poem, so I was hit hard across my hand. The fear of this retribution had a lasting impact on me. Through Loving-Kindness meditation, I attempted to cultivate compassion even towards this teacher.

That evening, as I went to bed, I experienced a vivid and impactful dream. I dreamt of traveling on a train back from London, which slowed down as workmen repaired the tracks. They urgently warned me, "Don't go left, you must turn right," repeatedly. The train veered to the right, onto gleaming new tracks with fresh sleepers.

Upon waking, I realized the dream's message: I needed to break free from the constraints of my past and embrace adulthood. Subsequent meditation sessions brought a sense of calm, as the dream had served as a healing experience. It was a powerful reminder of the mind's ability to bring about positive change.

A DHAMMA STORY

Rose was a 38-year-old woman, married with two young children – a boy and a girl. One glorious summer day, she decided to go for a long walk to reflect on things. She had a fairly happy life but was always troubled by questions about her existence. She had joined a local Buddhist meditation group run by a wonderful nun whom she admired.

Despite practicing meditation for a few years, she could never fully commit to it. There was always something else to do, somewhere else to be. Whether it was too hot or too cold, she felt tired, had a headache, or found excuses like watching another television program or indulging in a cake her husband had bought her.

As Rose walked through a beautiful wood with lovely bluebells lining the winding path, she suddenly felt faint and fell, hitting her head on a sharp stone. Blood poured down her face and into her eye, leaving her unable to move and in excruciating pain, struggling to breathe with loud rasping sounds.

After lying there for a while, she realized she had left her bag behind, meaning if she were found, no one would know her identity. Unable to speak and with darkness closing in, she lost consciousness.

Upon waking, Rose found herself in a hospital far from home, having been transferred due to overcrowding at the local hospital. She felt terrible and unable to respond even when asked her name.

On the other side of the bed, she could faintly hear a doctor telling her nurse that she only had a few hours to live, and there was nothing more to be done, except to provide the best possible care.

Her impending death weighed heavily on her as she thought about her family not being able to find her, leaving her to die alone. Her mind wandered to material possessions like her new Jaguar car and the move to their new house in the Cotswolds that would now never happen.

Regret filled her heart as she realized that if she had dedicated more effort to her meditation practice, she could have faced death with peace instead of fear and pain. The last thing she remembered were the tears streamed down her cheeks as the nurse gently holding her hand.

The next moment, Rose found herself floating above her hospital bed, looking down at her body below, unable to return to it. A flood of thoughts about her life, both good and bad, rushed through her mind, including things she had long forgotten.

As her husband and children entered the room, crying inconsolably, Rose wished for their grief to cease, feeling free from all pain.

In the distance, a bright white light beckoned to her, enveloping her with a love more profound than any she had known. It was a love beyond comprehension.

She recalled the teachings of Buddhism from her favourite nun about the Jhanas, realizing that in her detachment from body and mind, she had entered a state akin to deep meditation. However, lacking the necessary concentration due to her inconsistent meditation practice, the light and the vision of the Buddha gradually faded away, leaving her yearning for that fleeting bliss.

Her journey continued as she glimpsed a heavenly realm in the distance, its beauty captivating her as she moved away from the light with increasing speed, losing her sense of self and merging into a boundless, timeless presence.

Eventually, she came to a gentle halt, feeling a loving presence and warmth surrounding her in a dark, safe and secure place. It was a sensation of rebirth, bringing an overwhelming sense of peace and tranquillity.

Reflecting on Rose's story, the narrator emphasized the importance of diligent practice to shape one's future existence positively. Encouraging others to remember this narrative if they found it helpful, they stressed the significance of consistent meditation practice and learning from reputable Buddhist teachers like Ajahn Sumedho and Ajahn Brahm.

A few days ago the sun came out so I decided to go for a walk to the woods. I put my summer shoes on because it felt like spring was in the air and off I went.

As I neared the entrance to the woods it suddenly started to rain heavily, "Typical English weather I thought." I put the hood of my coat up which slightly obscured my vision. The next thing I knew I was falling. I had slipped on a wet paving stone. As I fell I thought of Rose falling over in the woods, now it was happening to me!

I hit the ground hard. My hands had scratches and stones embedded in them, they were bleeding. My knee hurt a lot, I could feel the blood running down my leg. My elbow was very sore.

I picked myself up off the ground, I was OK. I was very lucky I hadn't suffered the same fate as Rose. As I hobbled home people started to stare at me which I thought was a bit odd. It wasn't until I got indoors that I noticed that I had a big hole in my trousers with blood running down my leg.

I sat down in the evening to practice meditation, and I reflected on my day. Indeed, I had been fortunate not to harm myself too much. I also thought about why I do my mind training every day.

One of the reasons is that at any time harm may come to us and we won't be able to do it anymore. These are sobering thoughts that I pondered over. I relaxed my mind and body, the pain faded away I was happy and at peace.

My real home is not my mind or body.

THERE IS...

The mindfulness practice that I follow is called 'noting'. I note what arises via the six senses. I watch the mind. Is there fear? Instead of saying "I am frightened," I say "There is fear." If I have lust, I note "There is lust." This helps to break the habitual way of attaching to things. No one experiences lust or fear and the habitual mind disappears.

There is a sense of freedom from practicing this meditation. We try our best to let go as much as possible. There will be many failures to begin with, but it becomes easier after a while.

The mind moves at a phenomenal speed, but with determination and an open heart, we can catch glimpses of what is causing our suffering. Sometimes suffering goes back many years, but it is still possible to heal the problem. Having a courageous warrior mind is helpful. There are recurring themes that may happen throughout the day, such as habits. When a habit arises, say, "I know you," then let it go.

The more we practice mindfulness, the stronger the mind gets. The mind is then able to see very subtle movements in thoughts, speech and actions. The mind can watch the mind move before the thought starts to arise. If the mind couldn't watch itself, there would be no mindfulness and no freedom from suffering.

ANOTHER LOOK AT THE FOUR NOBLE TRUTHS

People often say about the Four Noble Truths that they understand them intellectually, and that is all they need to know.

1. All people experience pain and misery. Birth is pain, old age is pain, sorrow grief, and anxiety is pain.
2. The origin of the pain and misery is due to a cause i.e. The desire that leads to being born again, the desire for pleasure, the desire for existence, the desire for non-existence.
3. The cessation of the pain and misery can be found. With the complete non-passion and cessation of this desire, freedom can be found.
4. The method to follow to stop pain and misery is the Noble Eightfold Path.

We can come to the realisation of these truths in this very life.

Try to get into the habit of going to bed on time, waking up early, regular exercise, moderation in eating, keeping clean and tidy, and meditating daily.

THE MAN IN THE WOODS

John was strolling through the woods near his home when he decided to venture further. The undergrowth thickened with bushes, but he pressed on. Ahead, he saw a clearing with a makeshift bench made of branches about a foot off the ground. Seated at the end of the bench was an elderly man.

As John approached, the man smiled and gestured for him to sit. They sat in silence for a while before the old man spoke, asking, "What brings you to this part of the forest?" After pondering for a moment, John replied, "I'm trying to understand my purpose in this world. I thought being closer to nature might offer insights into the nature of reality."

This response was uncharacteristic, but he felt a sense of openness with this man that allowed him to speak freely without fear of judgment. The man smiled warmly and invited John to his humble abode nearby, a small, tidy hut with a cave-like room at the back.

A gentle fire crackled under a kettle, ready to brew tea for their conversation ...

LIFE'S PURPOSE

I have been blessed to have an understanding of my life's purpose at about two years old. This knowledge has been very useful in helping me through life's hurdles.

I look back through my time on Earth. Sometimes I ask young Richard if I am following the right path. Am I veering to the left of the path or to the right? Well, I think that it all comes down to the Noble Eightfold Path: Right View, Right Resolve, Right Speech, Right Action, Right Livelihood, Right Effort, Right Mindfulness and Right Concentration. Of course, he didn't know the Eightfold Path as such, but he instinctively knew when things were right or wrong spiritually.

He would show me a grassy path (in my mind's eye). On the left or to the right of the path was a ditch where I could get stuck. He would show me the centre of the path just by pointing his hand straight ahead. If I was caught up in lust or desire for material things or spiritual things, he would point his hand straight ahead.

So he teaches me as an adult, and I help him overcome some of his childhood traumas (believe me, there are many).

A helpful practice to look at is what is happening right now. Try to be present, for that is all that we have. The future never arrives, and the past is dead and gone. I often think and speak about this.

The skill is to be focused as much of the day as possible. I know I fail many times, but I keep on trying; that is the skill. When we realize that we have lost focus, then refocus; this is the natural way of mindfulness.

A MESSAGE FROM LITTLE RICHARD

Little Richard was alone one day in an infant's school when he was five. It was raining and dark. In fact, it always seemed to be dark and gloomy. Some teachers said the weather was so bad because of the A-Bomb tests in the upper atmosphere in the nineteen fifties.

He was sitting all alone, which was quite normal for him. For most of his life, he felt unloved. He didn't join in much with other children, mainly because of his acute shyness. Some of the children were fighting and generally being a nuisance. He thought that this sort of behaviour was not for him.

The room got even darker, and there was a huge thunderstorm outside. He thought, "What sort of place have I come to? This isn't very nice." As he pondered about this, he felt a huge, wonderful, loving presence around his heart and chest. It felt like it was enclosed in a cage. He knew this wonderful feeling would need to be released to help as many people as he could in his future life. He had no idea how this was to be done.

Richard, as an adult, never forgot this experience. It would come up in his meditation practice, mainly while practicing loving-kindness towards himself. He realized that being kind and helpful was the way to release this positive energy. Whether good or bad, every person in the world has this energy hidden deep inside their heart, just waiting to be released.

THE GUITAR

A couple of months ago, I made the decision to stop playing the guitar (admittedly not very well) and also to stop humming and whistling. I had arrived at the understanding that these habits were a form of compensation, allowing me to avoid confronting underlying suffering.

About a week ago, on what seemed like a normal day, I hastily ate a chocolate biscuit which became lodged at the back of my teeth. As I manoeuvred to dislodge the food, I discovered that my tongue had become stuck in a curled-up shape, rendering me unable to speak. This led me to worry about the aging process and whether my tongue was losing its flexibility, causing me to fear the possibility of losing my ability to communicate effectively.

During dinner that evening, I noticed that my throat had also tightened, making it challenging to eat and drink. It dawned on me that these physical manifestations in my mouth and throat were connected to my inability to express something important that needed to be said. This issue seemed to arise sporadically, leaving me puzzled about its root cause.

The following day, as I engaged in my meditation practice starting with mindful walking and then transitioning to sitting practice, I observed a dying flower in the garden, its rain-soaked petals glistening. I felt inspired to capture its beauty through photography for a local camera club competition later that day.

However, my throat and tongue suddenly constricted severely, causing great discomfort. I realized that the tightness was triggered by my fear of being criticized by a fellow camera club member who specialized in photographing dead flowers, suspecting that she might accuse me of copying her ideas. This revelation shed light on the underlying issue. Now, the challenge lay in how to address and heal these emotional wounds.

It is often said that when a student is ready, a teacher will appear. This experience served as a lesson, highlighting my struggle to assert myself and not passively accept unjust criticism. The wisdom of the Buddha's words, "This is the realm of suffering, but there is a way out," resonated deeply with me.

Recognizing the impermanence of every thought, feeling, and emotion, and their transient nature, I understood the Buddhist concept of arising and passing away. By observing these mental phenomena within my consciousness and letting go when they naturally dissipate, I could alleviate my suffering and attain a state of profound contentment. Through this enlightened perspective, I grasped that we are essentially pure consciousness, and all experiences manifest as movements of energy within us.

Writing about my challenges has already begun to alleviate some of the symptoms. The next step involves practicing loving-kindness meditation towards those who have caused me harm in my life, with the hope of facilitating further healing.

I look forward to the journey ahead and the possibility of feeling better soon.

WALKING IN GRACE

Today on my daily walk around the streets of Billericay I noticed that my mind was wandering. With the realization that I wasn't on the walk at all. If anything I was walking through thoughts.

So walking in grace or refinement of movement, taking great care in one's steps is a much better form of walking. The thoughts slow down, and happiness arises. The walk becomes far more enjoyable.

Breathing in grace with more refinement of movement allows one to become more in tune with the nature of reality. With every inhalation, you are born, and with every exhalation, you die. The moment that you were born the first thing you did was an inhalation. What is the last thing you will do? We must understand that mortality is the fundamental reality of our existence.

Are we wanting the next breath?

SUFFERING WITH NO CAUSE?

Imagine a person who has suffered a lot in life with anxiety, worries and fears. When this person enters a room, they have to open the doors and windows; otherwise, they have a panic attack or feel on edge.

Now, this can be helped or even cured with meditation practice. With mindfulness, especially in retrospect, the person can understand what has happened.

Are some rooms worse than others? Does the person feel more uncomfortable when certain people are in the room? Watch the mind!

The practitioner sits in meditation, working through the problem. They then open their human heart as best they can and ask why.

The mind clears, and they are about to get the answer when the ego steps in and closes their understanding. The ego wants to be enlightened but it doesn't want to lose. Sometimes the ego throws up something frightening or maybe a bad pain.

When I was going through this stuff, it felt like someone had stuck a spear through my heart and then was twisting it around.

We need to be warriors. Trust the teachings of the Buddha and have a strong resolve to understand what is going on. This can sometimes be very hard, but the rewards are truly wonderful.

So sit in meditation with a strong resolve. If the ego's protection devices arise, let go of them and don't attach to them; then the answer will be revealed. You can say to yourself, "I know you."

It feels like there is a door in front of you, but this time you have the courage to push the door open and walk through. You see your problem very clearly with wonderful insight.

The next stage in this meditation practice is to say to yourself, "I forgive myself for what I did on that day." Then imagine your parents standing in front of you, and you say, "I forgive you both for what you did to me." This story is fabricated, but draw on one from you own past experience.

The real benefits are that you will feel much happier and maybe the symptoms of a long illness will be reduced or even completely disappear.

NOTICES FOR MINDFULNESS

Many years ago, as a young man just starting my meditation practice, I found it difficult to maintain mindfulness throughout the day. To be perfectly honest, it can still be quite a challenge.

Around the house, I would place little reminders such as 'Don't forget to be aware' or 'Watch what you are doing.' Sometimes, I would lay a flower on the table to remind me of impermanence. I found these reminders to be very useful. Shamefully however, as the years passed, I neglected these helpful aids to memory, but am planning to reintroduce them.

Developing a quick and concentrated mind is essential to identify the causes of our suffering and find a way out of our difficulties. The mind moves so rapidly that it cleverly covers its tracks, requiring us to be vigilant to catch it in action.

For instance, the other day while eating breakfast, I experienced tightness in my tongue and throat, making it challenging to eat and swallow. There was a significant amount of tension present. By relaxing, the feeling eventually subsided. Reflecting on this experience, I realized that I had missed the moment.

Later, as I went upstairs to wash my face, a childhood memory resurfaced. I recalled my parents attempting to feed me some unpleasant-tasting food that I refused to eat. Each time the spoon approached my mouth, I would turn away, much to my parents' frustration.

After revisiting this memory, I felt a sense of relief knowing that I had carried this trauma for years and was now liberated from it. Mindfulness serves as a valuable tool to guide us towards inner peace.

PERCEPTION

I was recently walking through the woods, enjoying the serene peace and calmness surrounding me. Ahead, I witnessed beautiful hues of reds and browns that appeared as if they were painted. These colours then transformed into shapes resembling painted horses on a fairground roundabout.

I was so captivated by this sight that I stopped abruptly, trying to make sense of what I was seeing. It suddenly dawned on me that I was observing two deer standing quietly in the woods, perfectly still like cardboard cut-outs. As I reached for my camera to capture the moment, they swiftly darted away.

Being just twelve feet away from these magnificent animals was a truly remarkable experience that left me in awe. I took a moment to ponder on the profound encounter.

Although this experience unfolded rapidly, it felt timeless in its impact. By gaining insight into perception, the mind transcended the need for 'naming' and found peace. This added a new dimension to my perceptions.

Reflecting on a retreat from years ago, I recalled encountering a snake on the path that initially frightened me. After a brief moment, I realized the snake was motionless, and it turned out to be just a stick. This incident illustrated that our initial perceptions may not always be accurate, but they carry an emotional weight, whether it be fear, joy, desire, or aversion, prompting a reactive response.

When we engage in naming, feelings and perceptions come into play. While the 'name' assigned to an object may be fleeting, the subsequent experiences of liking, disliking, or claiming ownership lead to the arising of suffering, as outlined in the First Noble Truth.

AN ENLIGHTENING STORY

Sunita was an 18-year-old girl living in Northern India. Her father had died when she was quite young. She sat watching the television with her mother, as she did most evenings. It always seemed rather uninspiring. Sunita had been practicing meditation from an early age and was quite adept. She had let go of fear a while ago, so most programs with fear or suspense didn't register or interest her. Feeling a bit low and sad, she went upstairs to go to bed.

Her mother knocked on her door and asked, "Have you seen this advertisement in the local newspaper?" Sunita read the article. A very well-known Buddhist monk would be visiting the next village tomorrow. Sunita leaped onto the bed in joy.

The next morning, it was raining, but this did not deter her. The rain became heavy with thunder and lightning. She got her raincoat out of her rucksack and put it on. The path became quite slippery as she climbed up the mountain. She thought about her life. She had always been good at her meditation, understanding the Four Noble Truths, and experiencing stream entry, but the next stage on the path seemed so difficult. As she reached the summit, the sun came out, revealing a beautiful rainbow in the valley below. The rainbow started from the building where the monk was to give his talk. How exalting, she thought.

As she entered the room, the monk was sitting on the floor in front of the Buddha Rupa. She bowed three times toward him and sat down with other members of the Sangha. The monk started his talk by saying that wherever you may be in your practice, whether you are a beginner or advanced, never give up but continue with true diligence. Sunita went into bliss; this was just what she needed to hear. After an hour of sitting, the teacher sounded the gong. He got up and walked around the Sangha, laying his hands on each person's head. When he came to Sunita, he said, "You will soon be okay." As his hands touched her, it felt like she went straight through the floor and back out again. What a wonderful experience.

Sunita was so inspired by the monk's words, "Never give up on your practice," that she vowed to extend her sitting and mindfulness practice every day.

THE BODHI TREE

Vivek was a curious young boy who lived in a quaint village in India, surrounded by beautiful mountains.

One cold morning, he decided to embark on an adventure to the heart of the forest. Shafts of sunlight created dappled patterns on the forest floor as his footsteps crunched on fallen leaves, the winding path leading him deeper into the wilderness.

While walking, Vivek noticed a peculiar tree that stood out from the rest. Its leaves were heart-shaped and had a silvery hue. The trunk displayed intricate patterns, but most notably, the tree exuded a wonderful energy that seemed to resonate in harmony with the universe.

Approaching the tree, Vivek saw a weathered sign hanging from a piece of rope that read "Bodhi Tree."

He sat cross-legged at the root of the tree, feeling the energy of life around him. Closing his eyes, he listened to the calming rustle of the leaves in the gentle breeze. In the stillness, memories surfaced, imagining monks in saffron robes and envisioning Siddhartha Gautama, the Buddha, meditating under the same tree to unravel the mysteries of existence.

After about an hour of meditation, Vivek emerged with a sense of peace, reflecting on the wonderful experience he had beneath the tree. He bowed three times to the tree as a gesture of respect before collecting his belongings and heading back home.

EARLY SCHOOL LIFE

I attended a private infant school in Leigh-on-Sea. It always felt dark, foreboding and truly horrible.

Nearly every day, the headmistress would read from the Bible, sharing scriptures that often focused on death, which made me feel faint and ill. I began to realize that I was harming myself, so I started to observe my mind and made an effort to break this habit. Eventually, the troubles never resurfaced.

In religious class, they frequently discussed the concept of the soul, but the teachers never provided a clear explanation, which I found odd. Despite searching within myself many times, I couldn't locate it anywhere.

I consider myself blessed to possess an inquisitive mind, one that doesn't blindly follow what I've been told but rather engages in independent investigation, namely critical thinking.

One aspect of Buddhism that resonates with me is its emphasis on eschewing blind faith beliefs and speculation in favour of dedicated practice until understanding is reached. While Buddhists hold virtues such as loving-kindness, humanity, patience, and generosity in high regard, wisdom and compassion are perhaps most valued.

From a young age, I've always had a curiosity to explore things. I attribute these qualities to Little Richard, and I am grateful for them.

MEDITATION IS A WONDERFUL THING TO DO

Meditation is a wonderful thing to do. It's not hard; the key is to stop trying and let go. Meditation should be a joyful process. By practicing letting go, we are releasing ourselves from suffering. The more we let go, the happier we become. We will carry fewer burdens in life and smile more.

When people criticize you, you will suffer less because your ego is diminished. In my younger years, I was often chastised by my parents, school teachers, and other children. I would replay these scenarios in my mind repeatedly, sometimes for weeks or even years. It was strange that in this state of suffering, I felt safe.

I used to walk with my head always down, developing a stooped posture. I couldn't bear to look at anyone for more than a second; it was too painful. I became this way because it seemed that only negativity came from people, and I had no friends. I was terribly unhappy and lonely, often crying my heart out.

After attending a few meditation retreats and practicing loving-kindness meditation, I began to change. I noticed people starting to smile at me, something I had never experienced before. I wondered why they were smiling, and then I realized it was because I was looking at them directly, without fear. It was truly a wonderful feeling.

So, letting go and loving-kindness are practices worth persisting with. Approach them with earnestness and delight, never giving up on their transformative power.

LITTLE RICHARD HELPS AGAIN

For the past few weeks, I have been suffering from boredom. I thought that I had left all that behind, but it has reared its ugly head again. Life can become a real challenge when this sort of thing happens.

Other meditation practitioners will have different difficulties, but it is all suffering. It is not a pleasant place to be.

So what can I do about this, I thought? I tried letting go. I watched the mind so as not to follow the thoughts of desire. But all to no avail.

I meditated a few days ago and just asked for help. My close friend, Little Richard, popped into my mind's eye. He was walking along a path with me following behind. He stopped and graciously picked up an object. It was a small Buddha Rupa detailed in exquisite gold. He held it to my heart. What a wonderful thing to do, I thought. I immediately felt much better. He was showing me the Buddha within. Every human being has this deep inside their human heart.

I think that Little Richard is the part of us that I call 'The one who understands.' It doesn't matter what the name is as long as it works.

So try not to forget that this special place is deep inside us and can be found with kindness and careful attention.

If you have a small Buddha Rupa, try holding it against your heart when things get difficult. It may remind you of the real enlightenment that already waits within.

THE NATURAL STATE OF MIND

There is nothing much to this mind; its natural state is peace. But it keeps getting lost in its moods. One moment it is happy, the next moment it is sad, then it is in pain. It is being tricked by its moods. It's foolish. It needs to be trained!

So what we need to do is to watch this mind and grow in wisdom. We need to understand the nature of thoughts rather than following them. After a while, the thoughts lessen in their power (In my case, quite a long while!) The habit of blindly following the thinking ceases. There is a state of nothing, a state of freedom.

Maybe it seems that one is not getting anywhere; in fact, there is nowhere to get to! Then one day, when all the planets line up correctly, one comes to understand, so never give up! March forward like a warrior with a kind and loving heart.

HEALING THE INNER CHILD

My inner child was very vulnerable; he got hurt very easily. A loud voice from my father or mother would make me unhappy, causing a wound in my heart. As a child, I found it difficult to express myself; sometimes my parents didn't want to listen.

We can go and find our inner child and listen to it. The child is still there and may be deeply wounded. We have forgotten about the child for many years; we need to come back to comfort, love and care for it within us.

Play with the child. Can you remember five things that you loved to do as an infant? Visualize them in your mind's eye, play, and have fun. Encourage the child to play games. This is all part of the healing process. Take the child for a walk, holding its tiny hand.

Your mother and father were once children; they had their traumas as well as you. Your grandparents need to be healed by you as well.

This journey with your child can sometimes be quite difficult. The ego of the adult can put up some very strong defence mechanisms. Sometimes we need to cry, but our ego blocks this process. My father would say to me, "Men don't cry." So I would stifle the feeling deep down in my heart.

MEDITATION AND MINDFULNESS TO HEAL SUFFERING

I have just come back from a very peaceful holiday. We stayed in a house set in eight acres of woodland with a river at the bottom of the garden and a bird hide. It was lovely.

This peacefulness set me thinking about how we can reduce stress and worries in our lives. I reflected on some examples that might help. Suppose we are going to give a talk later on in the day, we might be concerned.

The mind through habit sends a signal to the stomach and ouch an ache (Could be any part of the body). We have missed the connection. We find ourselves with a stomach ache and have no idea how it got there. We feel like cancelling the talk.

The mind is very fast, quicker than any flash of lightning. What we have missed is that there is a movement in the mind, we then have worry, and then pain. If we don't see the movement with the thoughts and worries of the future talk it will harm us. The mind sends a signal down a well-worn route to a part of the body, usually the stomach in my case.

Through mindfulness, we can see the mind very clearly. When we have caught this movement and seen it with good concentration and a sense of letting go, we will be able to give the talk with no worries or fears.

The practice of mindfulness and meditation are wonderful tools to bring us happiness, so keep on being in the present moment.

THE LAW OF ATTRACTION

Many years ago I left my job and decided to set up my art studio at home. With a mortgage, my wife, and two young children to look after it was quite daunting.

In the first week, I earned £5.00 and received two phone calls. What have I done I thought. People would phone me and they would say "How's it going"? I would answer "Very badly I have got hardly any work".

I would go to the cash machine there was no money there. I became depressed and fed up.

The bills would mount up and I couldn't pay them. It was then that I decided to be positive. Friends would contact me and "Say how are you doing"? I would reply that I was doing really well even though I wasn't. I would make myself sound really cheerful. It was then that I was given a £65,000 computer to demonstrate from a company that I knew. They paid for me to go to Italy to learn how to use it. Later I used it for my photographs. The work just flooded in I was doing really well. No one locally had got anything close to this computer.

So in our meditation practice, the same rules apply. If we feel depressed or frightened that is what we will keep getting. The opposite of fear is knowledge and understanding. The opposite of depression is vitality.

When I first started my meditation practice it seemed other people always had wonderful spiritual experiences. I thought then "No lovely experience ever happens to me". No is negative, so that is what the universe will give us, nothing!

Try to be positive, kind and helpful in as many ways as you can, especially towards yourself.

PARENT MYSELF

I have recently been thinking about some of the traumas that Little Richard had when it occurred to me that as an adult I need to parent myself as a young child. We can carry many deep troubling problems from early childhood to the present day as an adult.

They can be really quite simple events such as "I didn't get a gold star at school today I have only got one this year lots of the other children keep getting them, this is not fair"! This feeling can continue into adult life. In every present moment, these emotions get dragged along with many others stopping us from being truly free and happy.

So we can parent the inner child by imagining the event, giving the child a hug in our imagination, consoling, and holding the child's hand.

What is so wonderful about this practice is that because you are being kind the child teaches us kindness as well! This kindness forms around our human heart so that we develop this love towards all human beings and animals.

Good parents naturally do kindness to their children, but maybe this didn't happen to us. So as adults, we can step in and do it for ourselves.

It can be quite a challenge to see what is wrong with our lives the ego can be very deceiving. Being unwell can be a big clue, especially recurring illnesses that seem to come around most years.

The universe is doing its best to point out that something needs healing. Does the illness go back to childhood?

If so try and get in touch with the inner child and the child will help you as well!

THE PRECEPTS AND GOOD MEDITATION PRACTICE

1. To abstain from taking life
2. To abstain from taking what is not given
3. To abstain from sensuous misconduct
4. To abstain from false speech
5. To abstain from intoxicants which tend to cloud the mind

To abstain from taking a life, one needs to develop a kind loving heart so that it is impossible to go through this action.

To abstain from taking what is not given one needs to know in one's heart the suffering it will cause another person and oneself also.

To abstain from sensuous misconduct one needs to know in one's heart the deep painful sorrow that can be caused to oneself and another.

To abstain from false speech there needs to be a knowing in one's heart how painful it can be to transgress this precept, for oneself and for another.

To abstain from intoxicants such as drink and drugs that cloud the mind. What is the point of drinking and drugs if one is trying to do a meditation practice to understand oneself? The effects of drinking cancel out one's practice for that day and maybe longer.

The five precepts can be found in many books on Buddhism. What I am trying to help you with is how important they are, in coming to the higher stages of meditation. If one of the precepts is transgressed it makes it much harder to come to presence and the first taste of freedom; to become aware of your mind.

Here are six tips to help with one's meditation practice.

6   Try to be really kind towards oneself and towards others.
7   Before sitting in meditation imagine that an enlightened being has sat in the very position you are sitting in.
8   Try and do a good deed every day.
9   Remember something really kind that helped another in the past.
10 Have a really strong conviction in the Buddha's teachings, this is not blind faith.
11 Try to let go deeply, not to attach, not to want to get something from your meditation practice.

RETROSPECTIVE MINDFULNESS

Now is the time to do a *metta* meditation for your mother. I forgive you for scolding me, may you be happy may you be at peace. In this retrospective healing meditation there will be many doors to go through, but each time you will gain confidence in opening them.

SO WHO ARE WE?

I think a good place to start is with the body. Consider when you were a baby. That baby must cease to exist before the five-year-old can emerge. There is no trace of the baby; it has vanished, so this cannot be me. This pattern continues throughout all stages of life. The teenager vanished many years ago, making way for a young adult. These transformations can be observed through insight in our meditation practice.

Now, what about the mind? The thoughts that race through our minds like a frenzied monkey swinging through trees, as eloquently described by Buddha. Can you grasp a thought and prevent it from changing? If these thoughts truly belonged to us, we could command them to stop or request only positive thoughts, but they pay no heed. E-motions – note the hyphen in the word – are always in motion. Do they truly belong to us? If they did, we could demand only positive emotions, but they remain indifferent.

So, who are we then? Despite the various stages of life we pass through, there is a constant feeling within us. I am not referring to the insecure child or the rebellious teenager; there exists an enduring essence that persists throughout our lives. This essence is not the self, the ego, me and mine, or the soul. It is infinite and timeless, discoverable in the present moment. By recognizing this, we can comprehend the teachings of Buddha and walk in his footsteps

WALKING MEDITATION AND THE MIND'S EYE

One morning during my walking meditation practice, a thought about my upcoming holiday at the Eastbourne beach house crossed my mind. What struck me was the image of the holiday home appearing in my mind's eye while I walked, despite my eyes being open.

This was a new observation for me. Although the image was faint, it was unmistakably present. Continuing my practice, I noticed how different images would surface in my mind's eye when caught up in thoughts. These fleeting mental picture often go unnoticed, but with closer observation, their presence becomes more apparent.

The mind's eye is a fascinating subject of observation. Consider this experiment: close your eyes and visualize a bright red London bus driving around Piccadilly Circus. The image materializes in your mind's eye, showcasing the remarkable capacity of our mental faculties.

Even more remarkable is the mind's ability to observe itself. This self-awareness is essential for liberating ourselves from the inherent dissatisfaction of life. Without this reflective capacity, breaking free from life's constraints would be an impossible task.

THE DEATHLESS REALM

Yesterday I went to Lake Meadows, a local park in Billericay, to capture pictures of the flowers. As I was photographing nature, I couldn't help but think that everything around me was in the process of dying. It's not a pessimistic thought, but a reality of living in this realm. Even the young children playing nearby would grow up and move on. This made me wonder, where can we find the deathless realm?

Christianity teaches that those who lead virtuous lives will find eternal reward in heaven. However, according to Buddha's teachings, the deathless realm can be found here and now. We don't have to wait until we die to find salvation and eternal life. We just need to look within ourselves. Although it's challenging, with careful mindfulness and meditation, we can catch a glimpse of it.

Life is short, so it's important to practice diligently. The flowers teach us that everything is temporary, so we should make the most of our time.

LOST IN THE FOREST

A boy was lost in the forest.

He had wandered too far from his village when he saw a small hut made of bamboo and straw. He approached and knocked, hoping to find help, but received no answer.

Tentatively, he pushed open the door and stepped inside. An old man wearing a simple robe of orange cloth was sitting on the floor. He had a shaved head, a calm expression and greeted the boy with a gentle smile.

"Hello, young man," he said. "What brings you here?"

The boy had never seen anyone like him before and was surprised by the man's voice. He wondered who he was and what he was doing in the forest.

"I'm sorry," said the boy, "I didn't mean to disturb you. I'm lost and don't know how to get home."

"You are not disturbing me," the man smiled. "I am a Buddhist monk and you are welcome here. I live in this hut and practice the Dhamma."

The boy was curious. He had heard of Buddhism, but he didn't know much about it. "What is the Dhamma?" He asked.

The monk smiled again. "The Dhamma is the teaching of the Buddha, The Enlightened One. It is the way of truth and happiness. It is the path of wisdom and compassion. It is the law of nature and the order of the universe."

The boy was puzzled but felt a spark of interest. He had never heard such wonderful words before. "Can you teach me how to practice the Dhamma?"

"Of course." Said the monk, "The Dhamma is for everyone who is willing to listen. The Dhamma is not a theory, but a practice. It is not a belief, but an experience. It is not a goal, but a journey."

The boy nodded. "I am willing," he said.

"Then let us begin." Said the monk. "Sit down next to me, and close your eyes. Breathe in and out, slowly and deeply. Focus on your breath, and let go of your thoughts. This is the first step of meditation, the foundation of Dhamma practice. This is how you calm your mind and prepare yourself for the truth."

The boy sat and did as the monk instructed. He closed his eyes and breathed in and out slowly and deeply. He focused on his breath, and let go of his thoughts. He felt a sense of relaxation and peace. He sensed a connection with the monk and with the forest and a new awareness of himself and the world.

He opened his eyes and looked at the monk. The monk looked back and offered a warm smile. "You were lost in the forest," said the monk, "but have found your way to the Dhamma. I will now guide you back to your village."

BOREDOM

PART 1

The other day I was bored, nothing seemed to interest me at all. This has been quite a problem throughout my life.

Anyway, something different happened this time. I sat down in my chair and decided to look at the boredom. As I looked it suddenly became interesting. Because it became interesting, it vanished, and as it went away, the feeling of, "I am experiencing this state of mind," also went away. I dropped into the here and now the present moment, it was freedom, if only for a few seconds.

This is all that we need to do so that we can understand who we are.

So give it a try the next time you are bored, or when you are suffering from another difficulty.

MOUNT KAILASH*

In a small village amidst snow-capped peaks in Tibet, lived an old man named Tenzin. He had spent his entire life in quiet contemplation and devotion to the Buddha. As the years passed, a deep longing began to stir in his heart – a calling to go on a sacred journey to Mount Kailash.

Mount Kailash, known as the 'Stairway to Heaven', stood tall in the distance. Legends tell tales of spiritual enlightenment and divine encounters to those who committed to climb its treacherous slopes. Tenzin's heart had a profound sense of purpose, he decided it was time to heed the mountain's call.

Along the path, Tenzin encountered fellow pilgrims – people from all walks of life, bound by a mutual determination. They shared stories, supported one another, and found strength in the community.

Finally, after weeks of arduous trekking, Tenzin arrived at the foot of Mount Kailash. He stood in awe at the splendour of the mountain, the climb ahead

---

* Mount Kailash is Asia's holiest mountain. At 6,638 m (21,778 ft), it is located in the far reaches of western Tibet. For centuries it has been an important pilgrimage site for Buddhists, Hindus and followers of the Bon and Jain faiths.

seemed daunting, but Tenzin summoned his inner strength, knowing that enlightenment awaited him at the summit.

With every step upward, his body cried out in protest, and his heart pounded in his chest, but his spirit soared higher. His mind focused on the teachings of Buddha, finding tranquillity amidst the physical strain. He passed out several times from the exertion and the chilling cold.

At long last, Tenzin stood atop Mount Kailash, the summit bathed in golden sunlight from the setting sun. Weary but elated, he gazed out at the vast expanse before him, the valleys below, the distant peaks dancing with clouds. At that moment, Tenzin felt a profound oneness with the universe, as if his soul had merged with the majesty of the mountain.

Descended from the heavens, an indescribable peace flooded Tenzin's being. Tears of gratitude streamed down his face as he offered prayers of thankfulness to the universe. He had found what he had sought – an inner light illuminating the path to enlightenment.

With new-found purpose, Tenzin began his descent, carrying the wisdom of Mount Kailash within him. He knew that his journey had only just begun to share the teachings of his pilgrimage with others, to guide them toward their awakening.

There is a Mount Kailash deep within our hearts, and it can be found through deep meditation.

BOREDOM

PART 2

For many years, I have occasionally experienced boredom without truly acknowledging it.

Just a few days ago, there were some mundane tasks awaiting me and, as I began work in my small studio, I found the familiar feeling arise. Instead of avoiding it, I decided to stay with it and allow myself to fully experience boredom.

Surprisingly, as I embraced it, the feeling of boredom dissipated. By facing it head-on, I found that boredom transformed into something intriguing.

I am uncertain if it will return, but I now possess a method to confront it. If you are also grappling with boredom, I hope these words offer you some assistance.

THE AMBULANCE

The other day, upon returning home, I noticed an ambulance parked outside my next-door neighbour's house. My friend had been taken to the hospital due to an infection in his leg that he had contracted while working in the garden. I have been acquainted with him for nearly fifty years.

The following day, his son visited me, informing me that the hospital was unable to save him and that he had only a short time left to live. I knew I would miss him deeply.

Today, my neighbours on the opposite side of the house were joyfully chatting in the garden about their daughter-in-law who was soon to give birth. Laughter and excitement filled the air in anticipation of this upcoming event.

In moments like these, I often find myself reflecting profoundly on life and death. I whisper words of goodwill such as "May they find happiness, peace, and freedom from all suffering." or "May they journey to a realm better than ours."

So as meditators, these two events hopefully stir us into a deep reflection, the rising and passing away of life and death. When we next start our meditation practice we can see that nature is showing us this event from moment to moment. As we breathe in the abdomen rises, stays, then falls, birth, life then death The body and mind are doing the same from moment to moment. Everything in this realm of existence is also going through this state of flux.

A FEW WORDS ABOUT DISEASE

THE DISEASE OF FEAR

When I was sent to senior school at the age of ten, I found it a very frightening place – in fact, I found nearly everything frightening. My father was stuck in the Victorian era and enforced the appropriate draconian rules such as, "Little boys should be seen and not heard," and "Children should only speak when spoken to." As a result, my home and school lives were terrible.

I was a day pupil at a boarding school and some of the teachers were sadists and their joy in life seemed to be in torturing the children. One teacher's special punishment, besides using the cane, was hitting pupils across the knuckles with a steel ruler. His favourite form of punishment was to lift a boy off the ground by his sideburns – one side only! Understandably, I found this extremely upsetting.

My parents didn't want me to enter the eleven-plus because I wasn't an academic child. I was hit with a cricket stump for not taking the exam by the sadist teacher. My parents never did anything to help.

Some children ended up in the hospital after being hit with a cane or a slipper.

One particular traumatic day for me was when three boys got hold of some fireworks. They put them in the petrol tank of a doctor's car and blew it up.

After the event appeared in the local newspapers, the headmaster called the whole school together for assembly to cane them. He caned each boy 26 times, I have no idea why it was 26, but will never forget that day as long as I live.

The culprits were boarders, and I felt sorry for them as their parents never visited them, even at Christmas. They had never been loved, so I understood why they were rebellious.

THE FLU VIRUS

As a child, I would catch the flu at least three times a year. It would often last two weeks and sometimes it was so sever I could barely walk. I was often in bed for over a week and would hardly eat or drink. Once, I remember having an awful taste in my mouth and to get rid of it I'd have to spin in a bowl.

The most interesting aspect of all this was that I began to see that my father was very nice to me when I was ill. I would normally be punished for anything, so being ill was an escape from the horrors of both home and school. My brother and parents never got the flu and there was no similar illness at the school. So, I began to realise that my symptoms were psychosomatic; my mind was replacing one set of sufferings with another.

This realisation was reinforced on a other occasions and the first was during a school French lesson. The headmaster had come into the classroom and explained that the usual teacher was absent, and that he would be taking the lesson instead. For me, the headmaster was a giant ball of fear.

He began asking questions and my heart froze. My fear was palpable and very quickly I began to experience all the the usual flu symptoms. I developed a temperature and my limbs began to ache. The headmaster asked me to translate something into French. "Please sir, I don't feel well." I said. "What a load of rubbish!" the brutal man replied.

When the bell sounded for the end of the lesson I thought, "Thank God!". I left the classroom and as I when downstairs the flu symptoms dissipated as quickly as they had arrived.

Another notable incident occurred when I was 15, and my GCEs were a couple of weeks away.

Every day, the fear caused my heart to accelerate, thumping in my chest and I felt it was amazing that I didn't die. My mind felt blocked and I knew I would fail my exams.

Meanwhile, a special trip to Canterbury Cathedral was announced and it was the only school outing that I had ever been on. The day went until I got on the coach to go home, when I started to feel very unwell with flu-like symptoms.

The next morning, I woke with a rash and the doctor was called. He couldn't decide if I had measles or not, so I was kept away from school during those crucial final weeks. I had escaped the GCEs, but I didn't fail! Neither my parents nor the teachers could criticise me because I wasn't there.

I have come to understand the intertwined nature of fear, suffering and the quest for inner freedom. In embracing these lessons, I discovered the transformative power of resilience and self-compassion, guiding me towards healing and inner peace amidst life's trials.

MY NEXT THOUGHT ...

Quite a few years ago I developed a skilful way to calm my thinking mind almost instantly.

First I would quieten the mind and the body by reducing my breathing to a slower rate than usual. I would breathe down into the stomach rather than into the chest.

I then watched the abdomen rise and fall, slowly relaxing more and more with every breath.

When I felt ready I would say these words:

"I wonder what my next thought will be."

My thinking would cease and could remain absent for some time.

I try to use these words throughout the day when my mind wanders into the future or back into the past.

THE NATURAL STATE OF MIND

There is nothing much to this mind – its natural state is peace, but it keeps getting lost in moods. One moment it is happy, then sad and then it is in pain. It is being tricked by its moods. It's foolish and needs to be trained.

So what we need to do is to watch this mind to grow in wisdom. We need to understand the nature of the thoughts rather than following them.

After a while, the power of the thoughts is reduced (In my case quite a long while!). The habit of blindly following the thinking ceases. There is a state of nothing – a state of freedom.

Maybe it seems that one is not getting anywhere, but in fact there is nowhere to get to!

Then one day when all the planets line up correctly one comes to understand, so never give up!

Go forth like a warrior, with a kind and loving heart.

THE HERMIT

Bhikkhunī Mutta was seventy-two years old. She had been a nun for twenty-five years and for about a decade, had lived a solitary existence in a cave in Northern Nepal. Her parents had died in a car crash about thirty-years before and with no siblings or relatives, she was alone.

Winter was coming and she walked up the mountain picking berries for her food store. The night air was closing in, it was getting cold and Mutta pulled her robes around her shoulders.

Back in the cave, she placed dried leaves and twigs on the ground creating a comfortable seat. With her back straight and her legs in the lotus position, she closed her eyes. It was a full moon and following the Buddhist observance* she would practice all night.

Nocturnal sounds drifted in and she habitually named them; that is a fox, that is an owl. She wished she could just be aware of the sounds, to let them come and go without naming them. She wished the terrible pain of arthritis in her legs would go away. She was suffering that night.

Mutta remembered that her teacher had taught her to let go, but she had never really mastered it. She understood the teaching, but the realisation still eluded her. She had been sitting for a couple of hours and the pain had become excruciating. What was she to do?

She broke out in a sweat and began to cry out in pain. Then, as the tears rolled down her face, Mutta realised that she had to let go – to give up – there

---

* In Buddhist traditions, monks and nuns observe the full moon, new moon and quarter moons. On these nights, they often practice sitting and walking meditation through the night without sleep.

was no other course of action. The pain flowed away as if soft wind had blown through her body.

The sensation of touch had gone and she couldn't find her breath. She panicked. Where had her breath gone? Was she dying?

She came out of the meditation with a jolt. The realisation arose that she had left the monastery too early, before her practice was properly developed. Her teacher had encouraged her to stay, but she knew better.

When the sun came up she resolved to return to her teacher and she set off down the hill to the town where he lived.

"Life is very short, at any moment it can end. I must not waste my time."

THE BUDDHA RESIDES IN YOUR HEART

The historical Buddha died over two and a half thousand years ago, but we can still benefit from his life by listening to his teachings.

We can remind ourselves of the enlightenment; The Buddha, is already within us. Realizing his teaching is a beautiful way to show kindness towards ourselves and others. We would not want to act harmfully in the presence of this great teacher.

Kindness and helpfulness can manifest in simple acts, such as assisting a worm stuck on the pavement or smiling at a passer by. These actions can help diminish the power of the ego.

As we continue our meditation practice, we may begin to identify many areas of our lives that can be improved. We can come to understand that there is an indescribable grace guiding us towards true understanding and freedom. By opening the door to our hearts, we invite true grace and kindness to enter.

WALKING MEDITATION

I benefit from walking meditation because it encourages my mind to become very still. It is especially satisfying to walk barefoot on the grass – there can be a real connection with the earth, like walking in grace.

We usually walk when we are 'going' somewhere, but when meditating we imagine we are walking in a sacred space; a space in which we move slowly and take each step with gentle devotion. We are not 'going' anywhere. Instead, the ground is cherished and we connect to it with each step. This way, we can train ourselves to be present and move with reverence.

To begin with, if you don't have much room in your house or garden, find the longest path that you can. People who have been in prison have used the length of their cell. If you are outside, find a place that is relatively peaceful, where you won't be disturbed or even observed (since slow, formal walking meditation might look strange to people who are unfamiliar with it). Find a path that allows you to move back and forth for 10 to 15 paces, around 20 to 40 feet. Place a marker at the start, like a stone or a shoe, and then similarly mark the other end of your path.

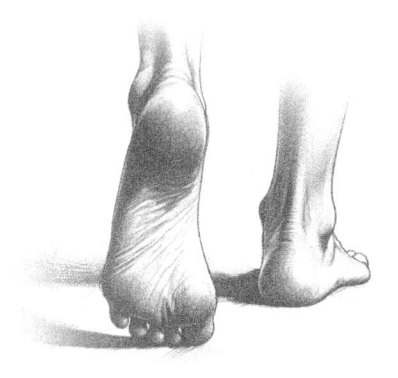

When we practice walking meditation we begin to see that it is impossible to take a step without first moving the body over to the left or right. Initially, there is the intention, then lifting the leg, pushing, and the feeling of touch as the foot meets the ground. Move naturally and at a regular and comfortable pace. When you reach the end of the path, pause for a few seconds, turn and walk back.

If you practice sitting meditation first, then walking, and then back to sitting, you may notice that each subsequent meditation feels quite different. You may feel more invigorated. Try it out and see.

THERE IS ONLY ONE CONSCIOUSNESS

There is only one consciousness but we experience consciousness through the senses. For most of our lives, we are constantly going outside towards objects in our world that we think are our reality. This place is subject to change it is continuously arising and passing away, it is in a state of flux. This state of sense consciousness can never bring lasting happiness because it is continuously subjected to impermanence.

We are thinking creatures, we have names for everything, and we project onto things. I like this I don't like that. Sending consciousness out through the six senses we create the illusions. So this consciousness is inside me. So is this consciousness inside eight-billion people and all the animals? This is the conditioned realm, this place keeps us divided, and this is the cause of our problems.

In Dhamma terms, there is only one consciousness which I call the void. At this level, we are all united. Meditation teachers say that this form of consciousness is infinite, there is no time and no space. It is a place where we can live forever and ever with no problems. It is the ultimate reality.

In your next meditation practice watch the breath arise and pass away. Each breath has gone forever never to return, it has died. Just suppose the next breath didn't come, would you panic or would you be at peace? Our clinging to things is strong, we are so attached.

As you progress in your meditation, you may find that your breathing becomes so light that is disappears. The sense of the physical body can also evaporate along with your senses. However, you should not feel anxious about this as it can be a natural manifestation of *samādhi*.*

So we need faith, deep faith that everything will be all right. This is not blind faith but great confidence in the Buddha's teachings. All will be fine it really will.

If the body and mind go the ego has lost, but there is something far, far better, so strive forth with earnestness.

---

* 'Sama' means equanimity, 'dhi' refers to the intellectual faculty and the power to "form and retain concepts, reason, discern, judge, comprehend, understand". If you arrive at an equanimous state of intellect, it is known as *samādhi*.

WE SHOULD NOT BE AFRAID

When you look at unsatisfactoriness (*Dukkha*), imagine yourself sitting in a chair or lying in a bed. When suffering arises, you may feel the desire to move to get comfortable. If there was no discomfort, you would not feel the need to move.

When a painful feeling arises in your mind, you might try to suppress it. It's common to feel uncomfortable when suffering surfaces and wish to push it down or cover it up. Instead, try to be present with it. Avoid running away from it by using distractions like drinking alcohol, overeating or other diversions.

Recognize and embrace your suffering, much like a mother lovingly embraces a crying baby in her arms. The mother symbolizes mindfulness, and the crying baby represents suffering.

As you realize that suffering can aid in your spiritual growth, improvements will begin to manifest in your life.

Understand that the ego craves enlightenment, but if it attains that realization, it will lose control. The ego is skilled at protecting itself.

For example, if you're working on childhood trauma and are close to uncovering the root cause, the ego may divert your insight to avoid losing its grip. Strengthen your mindfulness to overcome the thoughts that arise in your mind.

Practice is key – practice, practice, practice!

Our lives are short; therefore, it is important not to waste time indulging too much in worldly pursuits.

MINDFULNESS IS THE PRESENT HEART

Mindfulness is about the human heart. It's not about thinking, but really about the direct experience, this is where we see things as they truly are.

Our mental activity which is the endless inner dialogue, divides the world into an abstract virtual reality. It is like we are in a film caught up in the story – it is all so real.

When I was at school aged ten the physics teacher said that the world was made up of atoms and molecules. He said that the chair in the classroom wasn't solid. This really shook me up. I found this quite distressing. So what I was seeing was an illusion, a mirage of sorts. I couldn't sleep well for a couple of days while I pondered this.

When we can find the presence in our lives we can start to feel much happier and content with whatever life throws at us. So we try to let go of attachment to the things in this world.

This doesn't mean that we can't have anything, but that we try not to make it our main focus. The fewer things that we attach to the freer we become. More happiness will arise the more we let go.

We can come to see the way out of the unsatisfactoriness of life.

Mindfulness is the present heart.

THE COSMIC JOKE

Just before Christmas, I arranged to meet up with my brother for a drink at a local pub. We had communicated via email, and although nothing specific was discussed, I sensed that something was amiss.

As we sat down at the table he told me that he had lung cancer and was scheduled to have part of one lung removed. He then explained that the operation would involve a stay of three days at Guy's Hospital. I was unsurprisingly shocked by this news.

Unfortunately, after two weeks he was still hospitalised and too unwell to receive visitors. I had planned to see him one morning, but he had another operation scheduled that day. Thankfully, the operation was successful and my brother is now in remission.

This news has prompted me to reflect on the brevity of life. At any moment, it can come to an abrupt end or be prolonged through a challenging illness.

As Ajahn Sumedho once remarked, "Life is one big cosmic joke that isn't very funny." A sentiment with which I now find myself in agreement.

One of the purposes of our existence is to comprehend and liberate ourselves from the inherent dissatisfaction of life. Failure to improve ourselves leads to repeated cycles of rebirth.

To break free from this cycle, we must release our attachments and free ourselves from the constraints of this realm. The experiences of old age, sickness and death serve as profound teachers, awakening us to the realities of the human condition.

I HAVE BEEN REFLECTING MORE ON DISEASE

All my life, I have suffered from niggling ailments which I think that we all do, one of mine being cold teeth. This would last on average for about three weeks at a time.

When I breathed in, if my mouth was slightly open my teeth would hurt with a cold jarring pain. The experience was the same as if I ate ice cream or drank something too hot. Specialist toothpaste is now available to help with this problem, but the discomfort was persistent and quite often it would turn into a bad cold. It was all pretty miserable.

I also suffered from feeling cold, I would even shiver on a warm day. These problems just seemed to arise from nowhere. I just accepted that this was the way things were for me. For many years I had been practicing *vipassana* meditation (insight meditation) and *metta* meditation, (loving-kindness meditation).

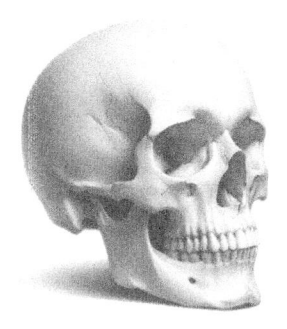

Before I began my meditation practice, if a pain or an emotion arose, I would not be able to see the cause, because I had not attained enough natural concentration. My teacher would say, "Don't let the opportunity go. Don't let it pass you by." I still failed. I couldn't see where the pain or the emotion came from. This was pretty frustrating.

It was then that my teacher mentioned 'retrospective mindfulness.' This was a turning point. When I struggled to see the 'root' of the pain and emotion, I would look back to the moment the pain arose. "What had just happened? What was I doing? What was I thinking?" This was a great help.

People would say "You know you are really terribly thin, they should photograph you for an advert for the starving in Africa." and many other horrible things. From early childhood, the teachings from my father were "Little boys should be seen and not heard," and "Children should only speak when spoken to."

This all made me over-sensitive and I just couldn't laugh it off. The teeth and mouth are the areas of communication, they became blocked, hence the pain. I wanted to react but couldn't.

Since I began to use retrospective meditation towards myself and my fellow workers, the pain subsided and has never returned. Where I felt cold towards myself, I now feel warmth and love and so no longer shiver on a warm day.

This didn't happen overnight, but took many years of work. I was finally able to see the insecure elements of my nature; my shyness, over-sensitivity and sense of unworthiness. Those places were the 'root' of the pain and I was able to see how they were directly connected to my physical over-sensitivity.

If you have similar problems there is a wonderful toolbox that you can use called loving-kindness, awareness and retrospective mindfulness.

Diligent practice is truly rewarding.

HEALING THE WOUNDS OF THE PAST

Until you heal the wounds of the past you are going to bleed. A person can try to stop the bleeding with a bandage of food, alcohol, drugs, work, sex or shopping.

But the real cure is looking deep inside the mind where healing can occur. The wounds can be healed with bandages of kindness and compassion.

Firstly, calm the mind the best you can. Choose a difficult situation from the past. Visualize the event in your mind's eye and make peace with the situation. Add a bandage of kindness to the wound.

There may be many bandages that have to be used depending on one's *kamma*. The mind may create red herrings to protect itself. The ego wants to be enlightened but it doesn't want to lose!

The journey can be hard but the rewards are truly wonderful. So try with diligence and grace.

May all beings be happy may all beings be at peace may all beings be free from suffering.

YOU ARE PURE CONSCIOUSNESS

To find out who you really are, you need to go beyond the self and ego. Suffering is not natural to you, but peace and freedom are.

Your mind cannot hold two thoughts at the same time, especially opposite thoughts. Try to contemplate the opposite quality of life. If you are feeling fear, make an effort to see courage; fear will subside. If you are feeling sad, contemplate gratitude.

The practice of loving-kindness will stop you from having negative thoughts. Every single thought or emotion is impermanent; it arises from emptiness, stays for a while and then goes back to emptiness. If you could just let this happen every moment, then you wouldn't suffer; you would be at peace.

Perhaps you have had this habit for many years of attaching to everything that arises, so the natural flow has been blocked.

There is a place where negative emotions do not reside; it is a place of peace and happiness that can be found in the here and now. It is everlasting; it has always been and always will be.

So practice meditation every day with great sincerity, and this place, which is you real home, can be found.

UNDERSTANDING INSIGHT 67 YEARS LATER

As a seven-year-old boy, I was extremely shy, introverted, and closed off to everything around me. However, as we will see, this turned out to be a blessing.

One day, during a lesson at school, the headmistress entered the classroom with a new boy. She announced, "This is David, he has just moved into the area." She then asked David if there was someone in the class he would like to choose to show him around the school.

Filled with fear and apprehension, I was certain that he would pick me, and indeed, he did. David came over to my desk and said to the headmistress, "This is the boy I have chosen." I felt unwell, as I had never been in such a situation before.

During the break, I attempted to take David around the school, but I could only manage to show him a small part of the grounds and classrooms before feeling overwhelmed. After our brief tour, we parted ways, and he returned inside.

I vividly recall that it was a beautiful sunny day as I stood by the school entrance in the playground. It was unusual for me to be put in such a position, and in that moment, I realized the need to mature and make more adult decisions.

Then, something truly remarkable occurred. I experienced a profound spiritual awakening. The trees in the playground transformed into a breathtaking display of beauty, with leaves morphing into atoms and molecules as if engaged in a cosmic dance. I was overwhelmed with bliss and immense happiness. This experience, devoid of time and ego, left a lasting impression on me.

Upon returning to school, I expected that the significance of this experience would be discussed in a future lesson, but it never was. Insights like these, whether experienced in childhood or adulthood, remain etched in our memories, forever fresh.

Reflecting on this experience, I now understand, sixty-seven years later, that by letting go of my inner child, I unlocked a deeper understanding. "Letting go is the key," I realized that by releasing the young child within me, I removed a barrier to my personal growth. We can learn valuable lessons from our childhood that continue to guide us in adulthood.

Reconnecting with our inner child can offer profound teachings and insights that resonate even today.

LITTLE RICHARD'S KINDNESS AND HEALING

The other morning, as I settled into my meditation practice, I noticed my body aching with intense pains of aging and the physical strain from the previous day's activities. Despite there being no underlying issue, the discomfort was extreme.

As I observed the pain ebb and flow, my thoughts drifted to Little Richard. In my mind's eye, he gazed up at me, offering a pure and comforting presence that brought tears of joy to my eyes, and miraculously, the pain dissipated.

It was the innocence and kindness radiating from Little Richard that touched me deeply. I pondered how these qualities may have evolved from childhood to adulthood, and whether perhaps Little Richard symbolized the purity of my own heart.

These are thought-provoking questions that we can genuinely explore within ourselves.

WE ARE ALL CREATURES OF HABIT

I have a rather silly habit; I love whistling songs. My father taught me years ago, and I've whistled ever since. However, I recently made the decision to try and stop. It wasn't easy, but I sense that I now have it under control. Was I whistling out of boredom or was it something else? More mindfulness was needed.

When I walked to school, I tried to step between the joints of the paving stones; if I didn't, then my day would not turn out well. We believe that this, and other irrational superstitions such as 'touching wood', can lead to good or bad luck.

We are all creatures of positive and negative habits, and it often seems that no matter how hard we try, we can not change those. However, by using mindfulness and self-awareness with compassion we can encourage acceptance and lasting change.

Remember the first time you had to dress, how difficult it was, but now it has become a healthy, natural habit.

The habit of driving is extremely useful because the brain's function can switch to automatic mode, allowing us to have a conversation with other occupants of the vehicle.

When we go on holiday, our habits naturally change to suit the environment, which is why it can feel so relaxing.

By reducing our unskillful patterns of behaviour, we can develop a less habitual, more peaceful mind.

THE BUDDHA AT THE END OF YOUR PATH

Every morning, before my sitting meditation, I engage in mindful walking. One particular morning, feeling tired, I noticed that my mind wandered frequently, straying from my meditation focus. To address this, I have developed a helpful technique. I visualize the Buddha at the end of my path, deeply immersed in meditation. This image helps to calm my mind, knowing that the Buddha is present.

Reflecting on how I would approach this mental challenge in the time of the Buddha, I recognize the importance of maintaining focus out of reverence for the great teacher. I strive to release distractions and let go of wandering thoughts. Minds have a natural tendency to wander, especially during repetitive activities like walking back and forth along a path. Thoughts may drift to mundane topics such as dinner plans or reminiscing about past holidays.

In such moments, I find it beneficial to summon the image of the Buddha at the end of the path. This practice serves to centre me and cultivate inner peace during times of difficulty. May you also discover a method that anchors you and brings tranquillity when faced with challenges.

I wish you an abundance of blessings.

WORDS OF WISDOM

I phoned one of my meditation teachers whom I still stay in touch with. I mentioned that I had been freed from some past kamma that had been a very big problem since I was five years old. She offered these words of wisdom for me to say: "I wish to be shown what needs to be known."

These words we can say at any time of the day when we need some understanding about something that has been troubling us for some time. This is so useful.

Please try this out, but it must come from a place when you have had enough and need an answer.

Open your human heart. In the human heart, there is no ego, no wanting and no desire, just presence, and then ask.

You may not get an answer immediately, but the answer will come if you really want to know.

THE WHOLE UNIVERSE

CAN BE KNOWN IN A

SINGLE BREATH

OFFERED FOR YOUR

REFLECTION

NOTES

REVIEWS

"Little Richard was a sensitive child who felt and saw things with an awareness beyond his years. Adopted as a baby, he grew up in a family that was strict and unemotional. Later, he met his birth Mother before she passed and a sister he did not know existed – happy times.

Finding his spiritual path through Buddhism, Richard went on to lead Buddhist groups for decades. This book is full of wonderful stories that will help and inspire others on their journey."

LIZ BARKER

"This inspiring and motivational collection of stories and personal experiences are written by the layperson for the layperson. A unique offering.

Richard writes honestly and with great insight on the Buddhist teachings of the path to freedom from suffering. 'Little Richard' had a difficult childhood but from a young age experienced strong insights, revealing to him that there was much more to this life than meets the eye.

Treasure this book, for it will help you experience the joy that life has to offer as we begin to relinquish the shackles that keep us from true liberation."

LAUREN RAMSHAW

THE MEDITATION OF LITTLE RICHARD

PASANNO BURCH

TEXT © 2024 RICHARD BURCH

ILLUSTRATIONS © 2024 NICHOLAS HALLIDAY

ISBN: 9798333900777

COVER DESIGN: PASANNO BURCH • R2DIGITAL.COM

PAGE DESIGN, EDITING, FORMATTING AND ILLUSTRATIONS:
NICHOLAS HALLIDAY • HALLIDAYBOOKS.COM

THE RIGHT OF THE AUTHOR AND ILLUSTRATOR TO BE IDENTIFIED
AS THE CREATORS OF THIS WORK HAS BEEN ASSERTED BY THEM IN
ACCORDANCE WITH THE COPYRIGHT AND PATENTS ACT 1988.

ALL RIGHTS RESERVED. NO PART OF THIS PUBLICATION MAY
BE REPRODUCED, STORED IN A RETRIEVAL SYSTEM OR
TRANSMITTED IN ANY FORM OR BY ANY MEANS ELECTRONIC,
MECHANICAL, PHOTOCOPYING, RECORDING OR OTHERWISE
WITHOUT THE PRIOR WRITTENPERMISSION OF THE PUBLISHER.

FIRST EDITION PUBLISHED 2024

Printed in Great Britain
by Amazon